D1337272

MY WORLD OF SCIENCE

Solids, Liquids, and Gases

Revised and Updated

Angela Royston

www.heinemann.co.uk/library
Visit our website to find out more information about Heinemann Library books.

To order:
☎ Phone 44 (0) 1865 888066
📄 Send a fax to 44 (0) 1865 314091
💻 Visit the Heinemann Bookshop at www.heinemann.co.uk/library to browse our catalogue and order online.

First published in Great Britain by Heinemann Library, Halley Court, Jordan Hill, Oxford OX2 8EJ, part of Pearson Education. Heinemann is a registered trademark of Pearson Education Ltd.

Editorial: Diyan Leake
Design: Joanna Hinton-Malivoire
Picture research: Melissa Allison and Mica Brancic
Production: Duncan Gilbert

Originated by Chroma Graphics (Overseas) Pte Ltd
Printed and bound in China by South China Printing Co. Ltd

ISBN 978 0 431 13769 8 (hardback)
12 11 10 09 08
10 9 8 7 6 5 4 3 2 1

ISBN 978 0 431 13827 5 (paperback)
12 11 10 09 08
10 9 8 7 6 5 4 3 2 1

British Library Cataloguing in Publication Data
Royston, Angela
  Solids, liquids and gases. – New ed. – (My world of science)
  1. Matter – Properties – Juvenile literature
  I. Title
  530.4

Acknowledgements
The publishers would like to thank the following for permission to reproduce photographs: © Eye Ubiquitous p. 29; © Pearson Education Ltd/Tudor Photography pp. 10, 19; © Pictor p. 28; © Robert Harding pp. 5, 24; © Science Photo Library p. 11 (John Marshall/Agstock); © Stone pp. 4, 13, 25; © Trevor Clifford pp. 6, 7, 8, 9, 12, 14, 15, 16, 17, 18, 20, 21, 22, 23, 26; © Trip p. 27 (H. Rogers).

Cover photograph reproduced with permission of © Getty Images (Stone/Jon Shireman).

The publishers would like to thank Jon Bliss for his assistance in the preparation of this book.

Every effort has been made to contact copyright holders of any material reproduced in this book. Any omissions will be rectified in subsequent printings if notice is given to the publishers.

Contents

Any words appearing in the text in bold, **like this**, are explained in the glossary.

Solids, liquids, and gases

Everything in the world is either a solid, liquid, or gas. Trees, rocks, and buildings are solid. Rivers and lakes are liquid, and the air is a gas.

Solids have a shape you can feel. Liquids are wet and take the shape of their **container**. You usually cannot see or feel gases, but we know they are there.

What is a solid?

A solid is something that has a definite shape. You can feel its shape when you touch it.

This toy dinosaur is a solid.

Each of these solids has a different shape. What shape is the ball? What shape is the box? (Answers on page 31.)

Hard or soft?

Some solids are hard and some are soft. When you press something hard, it does not change shape under your fingers.

This toy dinosaur is made of hard plastic.

This teddy
bear is soft.

When you press a soft toy, your fingers
make a **dent** in it. Soft things can be
nice to squeeze and cuddle.

Rough or smooth?

You can use your fingertips to feel if something is **smooth** or **rough**. A smooth plastic ball is slippery. A rough tennis ball is easier to catch.

The leaves of an apple tree are smooth, but the apples are smoother. The branches of the tree are rough – much rougher than the leaves.

Changing shape

Some things change shape easily. You can make many different shapes from modelling clay. Try stretching it and squashing it.

Some things can be bent into a different shape. A rope can be twisted and tied into a knot. The branch of the tree can bend, too.

Tiny pieces

Some solids are ground into tiny pieces.
Talcum powder, flour, and salt are sold
in tiny pieces because they are easier
to use like that.

Solids in tiny pieces are often called powders. They can be poured from one **container** to another. They can also be poured into a **heap**.

Liquids

Liquids can be poured from one **container** to another, too, but not into a **heap**. A liquid always takes the shape of its container.

When you pour juice from a carton into a glass, it becomes a different shape. What happens when the juice spills? (Answer on page 31.)

Thick or thin?

Some liquids are so thick that they can hardly be poured at all. Thick liquid **flows** very slowly.

The paint in this tin is very thick.

Thin liquids flow faster than thick ones.
Gravy is thinner than yoghurt. It flows
faster than yoghurt. But milk and water
flow even faster than gravy.

Mixing solids and liquids

Some solids and liquids can be mixed together. When you add some powdered paint to water, the water changes colour.

When you add salt to water, the salt seems to disappear! In fact, the salt has **dissolved**. You can tell the salt is still there by tasting the water.

Gases

A gas has no particular shape. It floats and spreads out to fill the space it is in. The space in the bottle above the liquid perfume is filled with perfume gas.

You cannot usually see or feel a gas. When you open the bottle of perfume, the gas moves out of the bottle. That is why you can then smell it.

You cannot see the air, but it is all around you. You can feel it blowing on a windy day. The air is a mixture of gases.

One of the gases in the air is oxygen. People, animals, and all living things **breathe** in oxygen. We all need oxygen to stay alive.

Melting and freezing

When solids are heated, they **melt** and change into a liquid. Chocolate is usually solid, but it melts when it is heated and becomes liquid and runny.

When liquids become cold enough, they **freeze** and change into a solid. The ice lolly in the picture was made by freezing fruit juice.

Ice, water, and steam

Water usually exists as a liquid, but it can be a solid or a gas, too. When water **freezes**, it changes to solid ice.

When water is heated, it begins to boil. Bubbles of gas form in the hot water. The gas floats into the air and forms very hot steam.

Glossary

breathe take in and give out air

container something that you can put things in – for example, a box or jar

dent slight mark in a solid

dissolve mix together and disappear in a liquid

flow move smoothly

freeze when a liquid gets very cold and becomes solid

heap pile

melt when a solid gets warmer and becomes a liquid

rough bumpy or uneven

smooth something with an even surface

Answers

round & square OR Sphere & cube — DONT MIX DIMENSIONS

Page 7 – The ball is ~~round~~. *Sphere* The box is a cube. *— Nonsense! How can one answer be 2D and the other 3D?!*

Page 17 – When the juice spills, it spreads out to form a shallow puddle.

More books to read

Change It! Solids, Liquids, Gases and You, Adrienne Mason (Kids Can Press, 2005)

Experiments with Solids, Liquids, and Gases, Zella Williams (PowerKids Press, 2007)

The Facts About Solids, Liquids, and Gases, Rebecca Hunter (Heinemann Library, 2004)

Using Materials: How We Use Water, Carol Ballard (Raintree, 2004)

Index